And When the Sun Drops

poems by

Connie Post

Finishing Line Press
Georgetown, Kentucky

And When the Sun Drops

*For Thomas
for all the words you could
not say*

Copyright © 2022 by Connie Post
ISBN 979-8-88838-056-7 Second Edition
All rights reserved under International and Pan-American Copyright Conventions. No part of this book may be reproduced in any manner whatsoever without written permission from the publisher, except in the case of brief quotations embodied in critical articles and reviews.

ACKNOWLEDGMENTS

Bridge Collapses into the Mississippi in *The Dirty Napkin*
Winner of the Cover Prize for Spring 2009
By The Window in *Carquinez Poetry Review* and *The Great American Poetry Show*
Autistic Son, Almost 19 in *Waking State*—Small Poetry Press 2005
Taking you Back to your Group Home in *Calyx*
Sunday Afternoon Home Visit in *Alongside we Travel, Contemporary Poets on Autism*
New York Quarterly Books

Publisher: Leah Huete de Maines
Editor: Christen Kincaid
Cover Art: Trish Fenton
Author Photo: Casey Henshaw, Little Rae Photography

Order online: www.finishinglinepress.com
also available on amazon.com

Author inquiries and mail orders:
Finishing Line Press
PO Box 1626
Georgetown, Kentucky 40324
USA

Table of Contents

Bridge Collapses into the Mississippi 1

By The Window 2

If Autism Had a Voice 4

Signatures (To your sister at age 13) 5

The Year You Would Have Graduated High School 7

Autistic son, Almost 19.. 9

Taking You Back to Your Group Home... 11

Charlie, A Boy in My Son's Group Home... 13

Last Day 14

Sleep Disturbance... 16

Blood Test.. 17

Seizure of Unknown Origin 18

Speaker with Autism Presents at Local Community College

    at 7 p.m.. 19

Getting You Dressed 20

And When the Sun Drops.. 22

A Letter in the Newspaper 23

Your Sister Ready for College 25

Non Verbal 27

To A Hero Twelve Miles Away.. 28

Cure... 30

Annual Review... 31

Your Sister Home from College.. 32

You Are Twenty Three Years Old 33

Sunday Afternoon Home Visit 35

"BRIDGE COLLAPSES INTO THE MISSISSIPPI"
Star Tribune—August 1, 2007

When the concrete
finally surrendered
to the weight of buses
and shallow moons

when the open sigh
of the river
swallowed its own tongue

I imagine those cars
and what the hard edge
of water
must feel like

years will pass,

the screeching will
make unannounced visits
on nights
when the river appears
to be sleeping

as I close my eyes
after the lamp goes off
I remember the day they told me
you would never speak

not one word

there would only be sounds

twenty years have passed since then

at times
I still find myself going back
to the elegiac banks of the same river

watching the water silently forgive itself
for not knowing
how to cease

By the Window

I used to put your baby chair
facing the backyard
facing the big pane glass window

you were tranquil and quiet
as I watched your spirit lift
soon lost inside the dance of leaves
of the tall tree outside

At five months you would stare
for what seemed hours
cooing at the melodic motion of leaves
your hands and feet moving
synchronized with each turn
of the tree's kaleidoscope of light

As the afternoon dripped down upon me
I found tasks to do, not far away,
and I would listen….
imbibe your gentle baby sounds
feeling certain that you would grow to love nature
knowing I must be doing something right
to have such a calm baby

I didn't know then
that the temporary disappearance from this world
was only the beginning of autism

It was the dawning of other worlds
of prisms that would take you from us
that would take language from you

It was genesis of a specific kind of spinning
that would yearn to make the picture whole, centered
to make the light
and its refraction seem just right

It is a time encapsulated in my mind
when I could not have known
where your silent motion would take us
yet I still cannot separate from it,
still cannot disengage from that time
when I knew where certainty ended
and began

yet, you walk in the living room today
a young man with brown straight hair
taller than I, slender and carrying a blanket
you've had since you were three
you go to the couch by the window,
cover yourself in warmth
place your head on the distinct edge of the couch pillow
and watch the leaves dance above you
on the trellis outside
adjusting your position
to merge with all I cannot comprehend

you smile in a satin and oceanic serenity
I have rarely seen in another
become immersed in the incandescence
of the entirety of this one day
this one afternoon
from which I cannot disengage
and I realize that you have grown
and have grown to love nature

and that as much as I have lost and found you
in all the waltzes of leaves and light
that I must have done something right.

If Autism had a Voice

It's not that I
grabbed your tongue
and hinged it to
the inside of your mouth

It's not that I
won't let you walk
straight up
in a forward, direct
motion

It's not that I make you rock
alone in your room

It's not even that
you mother still brushes
your teeth at night

It's that I've found this mirror
of the world
inside your steel gray eyes

and I couldn't find
anywhere else
to rest

Signatures
To your sister at age 13

you signed another birthday card today
another one with your name
and your brother's

you've been signing cards
on his behalf
his whole life

his autism
does not understand
the distinct structure of salutation

so you take your pen
write your name
and then his

script the silent loss
across the bottom of the card
center the permanence
near the bottom

then you hand the card to me
as you always do

as you approach the college years
I realize you will not always be here
to sign cards

it will be me
hovering like a hummingbird
on those blank moments of indecision

it will be me
who will hold each letter in my hand
I will enfold them into me
as if I am the envelope of memory

the seasons will come
fall to the wayside
birthdays will pass
cards will fall across tables
seeking signatures that cannot be written
and the memory of your cursive
across an unfilled page

The Year You Would Have Graduated High School

Is finally here

early June
a thick and merciless stack of mail
waits
I lay out the graduation announcements
college invitations
photo requests

the table is heavier now
needs more polish

The robes and tassels
of years crumbled away
lie off center

How can the thought
of a cake un-cut
bring me to my knees

I pace the house
as I step in and out
of floorboards of memory

I think of you far away
eating a dinner of macaroni and cheese
at your group home
with other boys who will never find
their way to senior ball

I think of the last time you were home
the way you came up behind me unexpectedly
and kissed me on the head

eventually, I find my way to your empty room
notice one big red bouncing ball
and a Fisher Price piano you've had since you were two

I look to the closet
where I've placed some of my winter clothes

making a silent space
for your invisible ceremony robe
between the steel hangers

Autistic Son, Almost 19

You are not merely metaphor
trying to take shape in a poem
not just stanza
attempting perfect rhythm or cadence
you are not formal verse
trying to make its way to a journal of prestige

you were home last weekend
I put away my journals
wiped mashed potatoes from your mouth
and picked up little crumbs of toast off the floor
where you sat for breakfast.

although I go to my desk again and again
I cannot seem to chisel out a sentence
that begins to tell your story

I cannot force myself to reduce your aphasia
to the very words you cannot speak

I put in another load of laundry
write sentences that disappear before my eyes
run upstairs again to make sure your clothes are still dry
you kiss me on the forehead
and all elusive alliterations fall away

A Sunday in October is over
the leaves in the front yard are turning color
along with the shades of your disability

I look outside
my words fall from old trees
scatter like thoughts

you come to find me
it's dinner time
your shirt is on inside out
I leave it that way

I serve baked chicken
while a kitchen window remains open
a quiet breeze blows
through the ripped holes in the screen

Taking you back to your group home

It's the same ride
fourteen years have passed beneath the wheels

one hundred eighty-three miles
round trip

I think only the road understands
remembers the fierce quiet
on the way back

I used to bring the green blanket
but now you like the red one better
the halfway mark is the truck stop
where the hay field ends

when you rock back and forth
the car moves and at times, you laugh
even then, people stare
even from lanes away
they don't understand that a car
carries a trunk of untold stories

they don't understand how many times
I've made this trip
pulled away from the curb
groped for my sanity beneath the seats

I have raged at the fields that have no way of
making it better
I have counted the road signs
when an hour was a place to drown

each town I pass remembers
the way you looked at me out the window
the last Sunday good bye
the way my chest caves as the water
rushes in

there is this one town, though, that has walnut orchards
where the rows make sense
It flooded last fall
It's a place where you grabbed my arm once, suddenly
deep in the teeth of winter
I looked back and saw you,
wrinkling your brow, leaning towards me

eventually, all the cars around us disappeared
the road fell beneath the silence
and the orchards looking on
telling us to hold on
to inhale this hourless road
and to just keep going

Charlie, A Boy in My Son's Group Home

One Sunday a month
I would make the same trip
the ending always filled with good byes
—layered regret

each time before I left for the long trip home
I walked across the room
to find you
in your same chair
staring into space
as if the blank air knew some way to
apologize for the life you had

your eyes fixed, far away

I approached
held my hand flat open
and you would take hold of it

your young, textured skin spoke to me
its silence
told me you knew
your family hadn't visited you
in six years

how empty the cove
of a palm can seem

I often ponder those moments now
six months have passed
since we moved our son closer to home

but I can't stop thinking of you
still looking far away
hands folded
as the afternoon
falls on itself
trying to find forgiveness
for having left the morning
too soon

Last Day

This was the last day
I will ever have to drive you back
to your group home
so far away

we have found a place closer
where we can see you
all the time

but I wonder
as I take my keys to hand
if the road will remember me

if each tree
each tiny bush by the roadside
will remember the scars that become miles

I wonder if the tired telephone poles
will tell the freeway
about the long curve of silence

maybe when the asphalt finally cracks
there will be a way
the blackbirds finally understand

they always seemed to ignore our highway
as they flew over the bent sky
landed on the dark grey power lines
lit the backdrop of coming rain

the clouds so gray—full with knowing

the birds deplete of the shadows
that come and go so quickly

it's early April
the trip is ending

you will be twenty one in a week
I make the same turn as always
find the same rough terrain of asphalt
just past highway 99
and feel certain somehow
the birds will come back
after spring has ended

Sleep Disturbance

The dreams when you talk
disrupt my sleep the most

the sentences fall out of your mouth
like water off a sheer cliff

I stand underneath the mist
and absorb
what I've always imagined
you would say

in the dream
I find out that something has
released the language center
in your brain
and all the words of years
flow out of your mouth

before dawn
I wake with cool drops of memory
all over my bed
I remember again
how it was never real
how you are asleep twelve miles away
at your group home

when I bring you home on Sunday
I walk through the house
pretending it never happened

but when I go into my room
to grab a change of clothes

I notice my bed has stayed damp
as if it has been baptized
by a river I have never seen

Blood Test

It is time to test your levels again

the same woman waits for you
in the same room

all that changes
is the needle

I think now you understand
there is no escaping
what they pull from our bodies

I think the swabs
the cotton and anesthetic
don't matter as much
as they used to

when the results come back
they will call and tell me
your levels are "a little off"
they will raise you
from one to two teaspoons
and the viscous liquid
will be given without ever
having passed through
your hands

Seizure of Unknown Origin

They say they don't know why
they start
when the next will come
when the electrical storm
will spark, swallow you

don't know when the lightning
the bolt
will push its way into your sky

what trees will split open
what fires will burn on the open meadow

they only tell me
try this medication

watch for signs of thunder

I am left scurrying
back and forth
between dry trees
soaking the roots with small buckets of water

running
so you can sleep
and I can give serum
in spoonfuls of worry

so the ground stays wet
and I can pray
standing
under trees
with no leaves

Speaker with Autism presents at Local Community College at 7 p.m.

Her words fall down the stage
into the crevasse of audience

It's 8:30 already
I look for a stick of gum in my purse
some way to taste my own words
as she talks of an inner world
a dark rain, an onslaught of harsh light
She helps me understand
why you flit your hands
and spin around in the middle of the room
for no apparent reason

she says when you have a child with autism
you must lose the importance of language
in the relationship

now that you are in your twenties
your disability changes shape
today—it makes more sense
why you screamed so much when you were young
hit yourself throughout adolescence

she does not absorb the dialect of your silence
does not watch me brush your teeth
on winter nights
put the toothpaste away, make sure the cap is on

She doesn't hear your noises
at 4:30 a.m.
the hymns of an unfolded prayer

she does not watch me get up
take your hand
put you back to bed
drop the language
back inside the covers
tuck it neatly
around your shoulders

Getting You Dressed

"Put this shoe on"

"now this one"

I say it as easily as "good morning"
I say it to myself even when I don't need to

I watch the way the walls
follow along the same script

for this Sunday morning
we are almost done

I only have to tuck in your shirt
make sure your pants are on straight

there is no abacus
to count the times
we have stood here

the myriad of ways
I have watched you struggle
to find button holes

the kaleidoscope
of fabrics you have refused
to wear

for some reason
I find myself thinking about
self help books that say
"one day at a time"

here I am
fastening one snap
at a time

straightening
your collar
one fold at a time

dressing you
one year at a time

we leave the room
with your unmatched socks
holding the same abacus
the same beads falling

And When The Sun Drops

You come through the front door
at six p.m.
you head for your bedroom
so quickly
sleek through the kitchen
past the dinner table

now that it is daylight savings time
I can't keep you downstairs
with us
no matter how hard I try

the sun drops below the skyline
and you walk towards
the perimeter of your room

as if the darkness
finally has agreed
to meet you
half way

I wonder what you dream about—
what stories your subconscious tells

if silence permeates your dreams, too
I wonder if you've ever spoken a word
in between REM and sunrise
if somehow I missed it
—if the moment folded into itself
and hid your voice
beneath the layers of an
unraveled dusk

I go upstairs one more time
shut off the hallway lamp
and wonder
if the clock I set back
is falling too

A Letter in the Newspaper
"This group home has no right to exist in our neighborhood"

How do I tell you
that there is bigotry in the world
hidden in neighborhoods
with white doors
and narrow streets

how do I tell you
when you can't talk
—why they will not speak to you

how do we walk down their sidewalks
and step over the cracks
the fears that split open like hatred

how do we find a way
to let the asphalt
hold more than the weight
of ourselves

the street
in its rough and black misery
may crumble when the
wheels of angry cars ride over it
but somewhere
there is solid earth beneath

I am not usually thankful
that you can't understand
so many things

but today,
when I open the morning paper
and see the scorn divided out
like servings of broken dessert

I am secretly grateful
that you cannot know this sting
feel words like thistles
from those who will never give you
your last cup of water before bed

I can only take your hand
find a gravel road
and walk with you
until the earth nods
and grants kindness, again

Your Sister Ready for College

You roam the house
more often
the night before she leaves
as if you understand
the rules of departure
as if you know
why the boxes
are placed so carefully
around the stairwell

her shampoo, books
pencils and thesaurus
are all packed

you wander the hallway
flipping your hands in rhythm—
in the only language you know

she sighs heavy
as the burgundy towels
she folded so precisely
fall out of the tearing box

I tell her not to worry
that you will "be okay"
when you wake
in the middle of the night

I tell her it will take me longer
to climb the stairs
but I will take you back
to your unfolded bed
before the morning breaks us

I assure you
she will visit often

but in the meantime
she has promised me
she will carry her notebook for you
each scribble inside
a word you could not say

Non Verbal

People often ask
"since he can't speak…..
"how do you know what he wants?"

which is often followed
with a moment of my own silence

how do I know when it's dawn

*how do I know when the fog
rises up over the eastern hill*

*how do I know
when Orion is stretched out
across the Autumn sky*

I hear your footsteps
as you come downstairs
before I am out of bed
on Sunday morning

each measured footstep
a far away drum beat
I have become accustomed to
in a dense forest
of silent blooms

To A Hero Twelve Miles Away
To Tom's group home care provider

It's not because
every day you make sure
six young men are dressed and bathed
—ready for another day

It's not because you make sure
they all go to the dentist and get check-ups
or that you drive them to Fisherman's Wharf
on Saturday afternoons

It's because in the morning
you straighten my son's clothing
as if it were your own

It's because just before I shut the door
I watch my son wrap his hands
around the crook of your elbow
and I know he will be okay
even after the sun has left me
and the house has gone dark

It's because I thought
I would never go to Disneyland
with my son again
but you drove for eleven hours
in a van with 6 disabled young men
and four staff members
and let me go quietly
on the Peter Pan ride when everyone was hungry
for dinner

It's because now when I drive up the street
and park in the driveway
I will find you spackling a damaged wall
or tending to the sprinkler in the front yard
perfecting the art of fixing what's broken

I remember the first night
when I had to leave my son with you
and how you let me call
as many times as I needed

I didn't know what he would be having
for breakfast the next morning
I didn't know what pajamas
you would choose for him to wear that night

but I knew that somehow
the twilight would know
and I could trust you
to see the complexities of its shadows

Sometimes at night when it's late
and the last lamp is shut off in the house
I think back to the first loss
how a diagnosis can sever the limbs of knowledge

how the phrase "group home"
can make the walls crumble

I think about how different a road feels
when you drive *to* something
as opposed to *away*

and then I think of you
and I think about my son
sleeping in his room twelve miles away
—how a life can be wrapped
and unwrapped in a thousand different colors

how one person
can make an origami out of
any shape of loss
and make it somehow
feel like gratitude

Cure

News headlines fill the papers
genetic links
possible breakthroughs closer
another article folded
and placed in the bottom
of my purse

I wonder if the next generation
might be spared

I wonder what other lives
will be folded
into these measured spaces

I don't know what scientist
will see the answer through
a microscope I will never touch

but all too often
I think about a mother
who hears the sound
of her young son tapping
tapping, tapping
the headboard
in the middle of the night

Annual Review

We gather in a small room
tables, chairs
half filled notebooks that try to tell your story

someone new assigned to your case
asks me questions
I have answered a thousand times

no he can't brush his teeth
no he can't make his own meals
Yes he tries to make his bed
sometimes he buses his own plates

sometimes he cries
we don't know why
sometimes he tears his clothes to shreds
—then we buy new ones

one hour and twenty minutes pass
each person at the table
closes their files

I want to tell them
how you said "cheese" once
when you stood at the refrigerator

back then
there were no case managers
no funds to be disbursed
no team meetings

just a boy
whose blond hair I combed each morning

and a silence
that knew which way
we were headed

Your Sister Home from College

You pace back and forth
as if the floor is telling you something

as if you know
how many miles
she has driven

as if you can imagine
what history books
she studies late at night

on Sunday
you eat breakfast at the same table
the crumbs from your mouth
fall
in different directions

I watch her scoop them onto her plate
when the meal is over

I watch you leave them behind

you kiss her lightly on the forehead
just before you leave the room

she reminds you
to put your plate in the sink

you have always shared this silence

as if it were bread

or morning

You are Twenty Three Years Old

People have stopped sending us the
"miracle cure for autism" articles

friends at parties have stopped asking
"will he grow out of it ?"

the science reports
climb out of the radio each day
genetics
environmental assaults
what's in the water
but nobody really knows

I keep my words sparse
so people can go on
worry about their own lives
parents in nursing homes
kids in college

the group home is closer now
you are home every weekend
I watch your sister learn to care for you
her tone of voice has changed
is tinged with mothering

I watch her hands learn to
fold things
napkins, your clothes,
unspoken needs

I step out of the living room sometimes
know you will be okay for a few minutes

unfold the mail carefully
sort things into stacks
that make sense

I'll be starting dinner soon
and although you've never told me
I know how much you love
the chicken I will make

you and I both know
how it must simmer
for the longest time

Sunday Afternoon Home Visit

I put a blanket over your lap
you need the weight of it
to calm

you flap your hands anyway
a flutter beneath the warm

you tell me you are thirsty
not with words
but with that familiar push
on my right shoulder

you've spilled the cup of water
I brought you
I get up,
walk past the bookshelf
with the alphabetical line
of autism books

I hold your hand
on the way out to the car
you kiss my forehead
then, I stand on my tip toes
to kiss you back

I used to think autism
was a war I was fighting
but now, I've taken up residence
in the small village outside of the
battle zone
and spend long days
beneath a cathedral of quiet trees

Connie Post served as Poet Laureate of Livermore, California from 2005—2009. During her term she created two popular reading series "Wine and Words" and "Ravenswood". She wrote 25 poems for civic and community events. The City of Livermore published this collection entitled "In a City of Words" and distributed the book to other communities as a model of community work. She has taught poetry workshops to adults groups and youth groups.

Her work has appeared in both print journals and on line poetry magazines including, *The Aurorean, The American Journal of Poetry, Atticus Review, Blue Fifth Review, Calyx, Comstock Review, Cold Mountain Review, Crab Creek Review, Chiron Review, DMQ Review, Dogwood, Mom Egg Review, The Pedestal Magazine, Pirene's Fountain, River Styx, Slippery Elm, Split Rock Review, Slipstream, Spillway, Spoon River Poetry Review,* and *West Chester Review*

Her work is included in several anthologies including *Alongside we Travel—Contemporary Poets on Autism* (NYQ Books, 2019), *Truth to Power Writers Respond To The Rhetoric Of Hate And Fear* (Cutthroat: A Journal of the Arts, 2017), and *California Fire & Water: A Climate Crisis Anthology* (Story Street Press, 2020).

Her Awards and recognition include the *Crab Creek Review* Poetry Award, the Liakoura Award, *The Prick of the Spindle* Poetry Competition and the 2009 *Caesura* Poetry Award. She has been short listed for the Muriel Craft Bailey Awards, The Lois Cranston Memorial Awards, the Joy Harjo Poetry Prize and the *Atticus Review* Poetry Award.

Connie Post has been an advocate for autism for many years. She has presented to many local community colleges and groups on the subject of parenting and advocacy. She has served as a keynote speaker for professional and parent groups alike. Connie has been writing about the experience of parenting a son with autism for three decades.

And When the Sun Drops received the Aurorean's Editor's Chapbook Award in Fall 2012.